THE *Writing* BOOK

THE Writing BOOK

How to write letters, projects, stories, poems, plays and much, much more!

by Jean Bennett

SCHOLASTIC INC.
New York Toronto London Auckland Sydney

Edited by Penny Scown
Designed and illustrated by Christine Dale

ISBN 0-590-43361-X

Text copyright © 1988 by Jean Bennett. All rights reserved. Published by Scholastic Inc., 730 Broadway, New York, NY 10003, by arrangement with Ashton Scholastic Ltd.

12 11 10 9 8 7 6 5 4 3 2 1   0 1 2 3 4 5/9

Printed in the U.S.A.   08

First Scholastic printing, January 1990

This book is dedicated to my family:
Owen, Karen, Alan, Raewyn, Stephen,
Andrea and Tony

CONTENTS

Introduction	1
Gather Your Gear	2
Ideas	3
Use Your Experiences	6
Write About What You Know	8
Short Stories	11
Fun & Fantasy — Mystery & History	17
Poetry	21
Drama	26
News Writing	33
Feature Articles	38
Interviews	40
Advertisements	43
Radio	45
Television	49
Process Writing	51
Book Reviews	52
Projects	54
Expository Essays	56
Summary or Précis	58
Proofreading	60
Preparing a Manuscript	62
Speeches	64
Letter Writing	66
Meeting Reports	74
People Talk	77
Writers' Groups	78
Recipes	79
Punctuation	80

INTRODUCTION

Have you ever sat down at a desk or table with a blank piece of paper in front of you, twiddled a pencil and wondered:

* What's a good idea for a story?
* How can I write a speech for school?
* Where will I find ideas for my project?
* What can I put in Grandma's letter?
* How do I write a poem?
* Where do I start?

Writing is all about working with words. Wonderful, wacky, wise, witty, whimsical, woeful and will-o'-the-wisp words.

This book shows you how to use words in many different ways and for different purposes. Browse through the list of contents and explore the ways in which you can make words work for you.

Writing is fun! This book offers you a few hints to help you enjoy it more.

GATHER YOUR GEAR

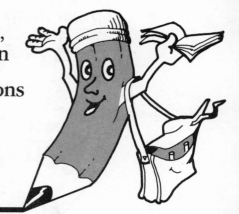

- Pencils, erasers, pens, felt-tips, etc.

- Notebook for collecting information, ideas and snippets of conversation

- Jotter pad for rough copy and revisions

- Dictionary

- Exercise book for finished work

Optional Extras

Encyclopedia — useful for checking facts and finding information

Thesaurus — lists alternative words that have a similar meaning, e.g., **sleepy:** drowsy, dull, sluggish, lethargic . . .

Typewriter — useful but not essential

IDEAS

Where do ideas and inspiration come from? Try these suggestions to get your creative juices flowing.

Sharpen Your Senses

Take your notebook and sit outside with your eyes shut:

HEAR   birds, insects, traffic, lawn mowers, etc.

SMELL   the fruit trees, flowers, burning rubbish, cooking smells, etc.

TASTE   a blade of grass, fresh air, salt sea spray, etc.

FEEL   the breeze on your face, the cat brushing against you, the stones under your feet, etc.

Open your eyes and

SEE   the world, its light, shade, colour and movement.

WRITE DOWN your sensations while they're fresh.

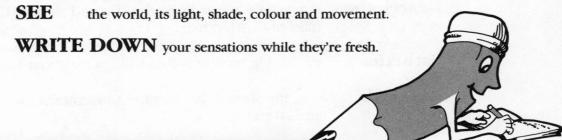

Stop, Look, Listen

At a bus stop, in the classroom, at swimming pools, in picture theatre lines, on a train, at sports matches, at the beach, on the street, up town, down town, at flea-markets . . . anywhere people gather.

Take note of the:

Amusing: e.g., a very portly gentleman walking a tiny Chihuahua on a leash.

Unusual: e.g., a well-dressed businesswoman riding a rusty old bicycle.

Sad: e.g., an upset child separated from his parents in a busy department store.

Descriptive: e.g., a baby's hair lit by the sun and shining like a halo of thistledown.

Pathetic: e.g., a dog so thin it looks like a cardboard cut-out.

Physical: e.g., the slow, lithe, languid movements of a waking and stretching cat.

Tune into often-heard conversation teasers, such as:

Jot down in your notebook anything of interest that you see and hear. You'll find characters for your stories, perhaps hear a good plot, and you'll sharpen the description of your settings with realistic details.

USE YOUR EXPERIENCES

Keep a Diary

Develop the writing habit by keeping a diary. Have you ever said to yourself, "I'll never forget this day as long as I live," and later realised you have only a hazy memory of events?

A written record of where you went, who you met, what happened and how you felt, will bring the day back to you. Record sights, sounds, smells and small details. When you use the experience later in your writing it will seem alive.

Write Letters

Write to friends far away, favourite authors, the Prime Minister, etc. Get a pen friend from another country. Make a copy of your own letters and keep the replies that you receive. Interesting letters are useful for story ideas and background information.

E-x-p-a-n-d Your World

Read the newspaper for human interest stories such as:

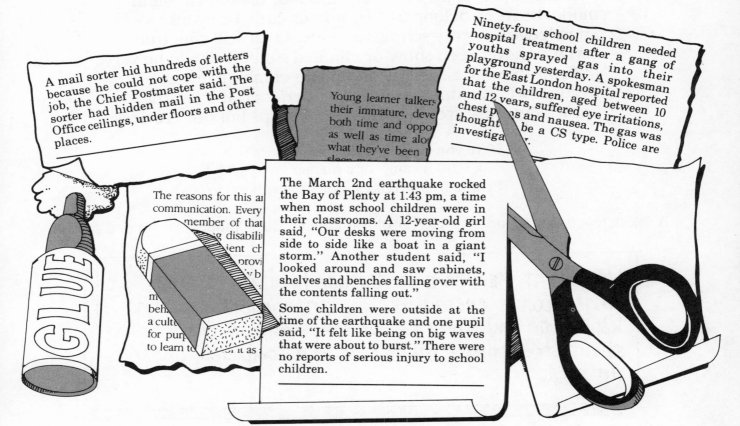

A mail sorter hid hundreds of letters because he could not cope with the job, the Chief Postmaster said. The sorter had hidden mail in the Post Office ceilings, under floors and other places.

Ninety-four school children needed hospital treatment after a gang of youths sprayed gas into their playground yesterday. A spokesman for the East London hospital reported that the children, aged between 10 and 12 years, suffered eye irritations, chest p??s and nausea. The gas was thought?? be a CS type. Police are investiga????.

Young learner talkers deve their immature, deve both time and oppor as well as time alo what they've been sleep m?? ?

The reasons for this a communication. Every member of that g disabili ient ch prov v b beh a cult for pur to learn t? ?it as

The March 2nd earthquake rocked the Bay of Plenty at 1:43 pm, a time when most school children were in their classrooms. A 12-year-old girl said, "Our desks were moving from side to side like a boat in a giant storm." Another student said, "I looked around and saw cabinets, shelves and benches falling over with the contents falling out."

Some children were outside at the time of the earthquake and one pupil said, "It felt like being on big waves that were about to burst." There were no reports of serious injury to school children.

GLUE

WRITE ABOUT WHAT YOU KNOW

You might play tennis, cricket or indoor basketball; build model boats or belong to a computer club. Use your knowledge for story settings and ideas that will ring true. If you've never seen snow or climbed a cliff it would be very difficult to write a credible mountain-climbing drama. Readers will see through your inexperience and lack of knowledge. Research can cover some gaps but not crevices.

Have you been to a flea market,
a school camp or a marae?
People like to read about what others do.

A self-defence course for 7- to 12-year-olds produced these thoughts from one person:

We learnt that the best reaction to attack is anger. Anger pumps energy into the very fingertips, adding kapow to any elbow jab or foot stomp. A bloodcurdling shout strengthens the emotion and completely unnerves an attacker.

Even if you haven't been anywhere or done anything, you *have* got out of bed each morning, washed, dressed, had breakfast and begun another day. Write about that:

I think it must have been my nose that woke up first.

The smell of bacon cooking drifted into my consciousness conjuring up mind pictures of Sunday breakfast. My eyes began to twitch beneath their lids, then, ever so slowly, they opened to greet the day...

Do you hate cleaning your room, making your bed or leaving the safety of home? Write about why you hate it and how you handle the problem. Do you love experimenting in the kitchen, training your puppy, helping with younger brothers or sisters? Share your experience by writing about your failures and successes.

If you have a special ability or disability, use that experience too. A disabled person can give guidelines on how to overcome problems and make the most of abilities.

Above all, enjoy your writing.

SHORT STORIES

Now you have a notebook loaded with story ideas, setting and characters — what next?

Characters

Get to know your main character well. Picture what he/she looks like, and be sensitive to his/her thoughts and feelings.

Write down a complete character list:

age, height, colour of hair and eyes, likes, dislikes, work, school, family, friends, hobbies and unusual behavioural habits (e.g., coughs before speaking, or rubs finger down side of nose when thinking).

freckles across nose which he feels is too big

taps his fingers when nervous

loves football

Choose a name to suit your character as this can be a description in itself. John will be quite a different person from Jack or Jock, even though they are just different versions of the same name. Manu, Helga, Hank and Antonio may give clues to the person's country of origin. Nicknames such as Shorty, Lofty, Swot and Freckles, give immediate description.

Give your characters different personalities and skills. If your main character is shy and hopeless at sports another character may be an outgoing, athletic type. By the use of contrast your story will be able to show that your main character has other admirable qualities.

Describe your characters through the action of your story. Suppose David goes to Intermediate School, wears glasses and dislikes his classmate, Rebecca. You could say all that like this:

```
David joined the Form I line.  Rebecca caught his
eye and David glared over his glasses at her.
```

Villains are fun. You can enjoy creating mean and ornery characters then have the satisfaction of giving them a hard time. Keep in mind, however, that rarely is anyone *totally* evil, so have your lunch-box thief throw crusts to the seagulls, or give your cranky neighbour a soft spot.

Point of View

You need to decide through whose eyes the story is going to be told.

First Person:

This point of view uses the personal pronoun 'I' when *one character narrates the story*. For example:

I sensed danger as I moved through the darkened house. I wondered where Andrew and Ben had disappeared to . . .

Third Person:

This point of view uses impersonal pronouns, i.e., he/she, him/her, them/they, etc. Although the story *centres on one character*, the reader is aware of what is happening to all characters through the third person narration. For example:

> Josie sensed danger as she moved through the darkened house, unaware that Ben and Andrew were trapped in the cellar . . .

The All-seeing Eye:

This point of view also uses impersonal pronouns as in the third person. The main difference is that *several characters are given equal importance* and the reader learns how the same event may have a different effect on each character. For example, one chapter may begin:

> Josie sensed danger as she moved through the darkened house, unaware . . .

The following chapter could begin:

> Meanwhile, in the dark cellar, Andrew leaned against what felt like a wall. He cried out as . . .

And then the next chapter might start:

> At the sound of Andrew's shout, Ben called out, "Andrew! Where are you?" There was no reply. Ben crawled . . .

Outline

Plan your story by making a rough outline of the plot. Your main character must have some sort of problem and will run into difficulties as he/she tries to find a solution. Through the process of overcoming these obstacles your story builds tension. All action should lead to the climax.

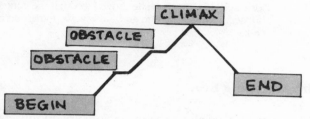

Phew!

Intense emotions and dramatic events are exhausting. It's like climbing stairs — sometimes you need to stop at a landing to catch your breath. Give your reader a short break by slowing the pace after each obstacle.

Bait Your Hook

Catch your readers' interest with a 'hook' opening to keep them reading.

For example: "Hey! What do you think you're doing?"

or: It quivered, moaned, and rose before her.

Introduce your main character and the central problem right away. Conversation attracts attention and leads straight into the plot.

For example: "I'm sure I put my sandals down here," Barney muttered.
"Mum'll kill me if I go home without them."

Action!

Put life into your writing. **This is often helped by the use of metaphors such as:**
Gleaming blackballs winked down from jars on the shelf.
The river snaked through the valley.
He heard the whisper of the wind urge him on.

Instead of:
Andy came home from school.

try something like:
The door banged and Andy shouted, "I'm home!"

Instead of:
Aunt Mary had a strangely beautiful brooch on her dress.

try something like:
The brooch gleamed on Aunt Mary's dress like the glinting eye of an all-knowing cat.

Conversation

Speech moves a story along without the need for too many details.

Compare:
They were very tired so they got ready for bed and turned out the light.

with:
"I'm tired."
"Where's my pyjamas?"
"Turn that light off!"

Speech can also be used to describe your characters.

For example: "I wish I was tall like you." **or:** "What a beautiful black eye!"

Don't give your characters long speeches, however. Two or three sentences is enough. READ ALOUD what your characters say — does it sound natural? Remember, our speech is usually full of contractions, e.g., won't, haven't, where've ya been, etc. Avoid overworked words and catch phrases such as: choice, go for it, etc. They will soon sound rather silly.

Climax

You've built up dramatic tension throughout your story and now you've reached the high point, the *climax*. This is your main character's moment of truth, it's time to stand firm and do battle.

Your main character must leap over hurdles on his or her own steam.

A convenient earthquake must not knock out the opposition nor should the arrival of help in the nick of time be used as a convenient solution. Rather, through trials and tribulations your main character has changed and is able to work out a logical solution.

Wrap It Up

Give your reader the satisfaction of a believable ending. It needn't be happy but it must be satisfying. Even if your ending has pain in parting with things of the past, the future should hold hope. Tie up any loose ends without long explanations.

Title

A title is like a signpost. It should be brief and eye-catching. It tells a little about the story but doesn't give too much away. For example:

Accidental Meetings — experiences of a careless cyclist

A Bed's-eye View — bedridden person sees life through a window

Survival — adventure story

~~Write~~ Rewrite

You're not finished yet! Now that the white-hot heat of inspiration has cooled, put your story away for a week or two. Then re-read it. You'll notice faults with the writing, see spelling errors and discover ways to improve the plot. Be firm with parts that ramble on and hold up the action. **Wipe 'em out.**

FUN & FANTASY
MYSTERY & HISTORY

Fun

What makes you laugh? Is it Garfield, Roald Dahl books, mishaps, sudden noises at solemn occasions or someone else's mistakes? Humour can come from your own life if you look at the funny side of everyday events. Study the drama in your own household and see if it has an amusing aspect. People in the midst of crisis will often say something like, "If I don't laugh about it, I'll cry!"

Mark Twain said, *"There are several kinds of stories but only one difficult kind — the humorous."*

Fantasy

Fantasy comes in many forms. For example:

Mystery, suspense and intrigue abound in all good fantasy tales. When you read them, notice that although strange things happen, they are still believable. You can enter the story and experience the magic too.

> Amy loved to watch the liquid movement of colours spread across the shining opal. She felt drawn into the whirling, swirling pool of light.

Let your imagination soar. Turn reality upside down and create the weird and wonderful. Have fun, but remember that the basic rules of good writing still apply. Get to know your main character and plot an outline for your flight into fantasy.

Mystery

When writing mystery stories the plot can get thicker and thicker but the end is nowhere in sight. The writer feels desperate wondering how to untie all the knotty problems. One way to avoid the tangled web is to:

Start with the end The mystery is solved, the culprit apprehended, or the treasure discovered.

Then work out

WHO DID IT? Decide on your main character's role. Is he hot on the trail of justice or wrongfully accused? You will need other characters to cloak in mystery or suspicion.

WHY? What was the reason or motive for the misdeed? Greed, revenge, envy, power . . .?

WHERE? The mystery needs a setting, a background.

WHEN? Timing and pace is vital in suspense.

Plant clues For example, if an unknown relative is to arrive at the end, establish a mysterious family history early in the story.

If a deserted house is razed to the ground, was candlelight earlier seen flickering through the windows?

If an axe is used as a weapon, make a previous mention of a chopping block in the yard.

Hint Tempt your reader with hints that will have them guessing what might happen next. Always be realistic. If a reader thinks, 'Oh, that couldn't possibly happen,' then the whole story is spoiled.

Create atmosphere A suspense story benefits from an eerie atmosphere, e.g., 'She felt an unease about the old house. The hall rustled with the movement of the day, alive with the lingering presence of people. Whispered scraps of conversation hung in the air . . .'

Check your facts If a character takes a plane from Auckland to Adelaide you need to check with an airline booking office to see if there is such a flight. If a computer hack breaks into police records, you need to find out if it's possible.

History

To really feel part of another time and write about it realistically, requires a lot of research. The best place to start is at your library. Ask a librarian for help. Many old books aren't kept on view. You will need to read more than one or two books on past events to get a balanced viewpoint.

It is difficult to write about history without writing about people. Shake the dust off old history books, blow away the cobwebs and get to know people who fought for their rights, their families and sometimes their lives.
To find information on local history, there are many avenues to follow:

— Visit your local newspaper and ask to see old copies of papers.
— Ask to speak with the library's archivist who will know where to find old documents, photos, diaries, etc.
— Churches keep records of births, marriages and deaths.
— Walk around the cemetery — headstones sometimes tell fascinating tales.
— Schools usually have interesting records about past pupils.
— Local government departments keep records of meetings and all sorts of things concerning land and buildings, etc., in the community.
— Talk with older people who may have interesting stories to tell.

Read about the era you're writing about: transport, housing, clothing, food, education, employment. Absorb the feeling of the time. Although people may have spoken differently, don't try to recreate Ye Olde English, it's very difficult to read. Clear, plain speech is best.

Visit museums that have historical displays; soak up the atmosphere. Remember, history is people. Breathe life into your characters. Recreate their joys, sorrows and achievements. Tell their history (or her-story) with great care.

POETRY

Poems can paint powerful, sharp pictures using images and emotive language which stimulate the senses. Modern poetry (free verse) doesn't need to rhyme but it should have a rhythm. Read aloud poems that you like, listen to how they sound and hear the rise and fall of their speech patterns.

Poems can be about any subject.

A bad-tempered breeze
drags brittle leaves from branches
to toss at the moon.

Whispy genies rise
from steaming mugs of cocoa
to stir the senses.

When I hear music
my toes wriggle
my ears twitch
my hands jiggle
my feet itch
Then I
. . . dance

Poetry may be written about windsurfing, exams, pets, computers, hunger, friends, dish-washing, camping, eggs, dreams, relatives, pain, insects, joy, smells, space, teachers . . .

Capture a Poem

Writing a poem is like trying to touch music. Music floats on the air but when you reach for it . . .

With your notebook as a constant companion, capture the feelings, thoughts and sights that crowd your world. How you see them will be unique. Each person has a different point of view and your vision is your own. Write down what you see and feel while it is fresh. This will be the core of your poem.

Listen To It

Take your notebook to a quiet place and empty your mind of all distractions. Read over your words, recapture your feelings and listen to your poem begin to form. Don't force it — hold back until you feel the words ring true. Shape or style doesn't matter at this stage.

Now let your poem rest for a while.

Shape It

When you return to your poem, the pieces will fall into place like a kaleidoscope pattern. You will see how the lines can be shaped into verses and the verses can be formed into a beginning, middle and end.

Make It Sing

By now your poem is probably a little work-worn and fuzzy. This is the time to get rid of any clutter and give it some zing.

Rewrite your poem onto a fresh sheet of paper and look at it with a critical eye. Are there too many 'ands', 'buts' or adjectives? Are some words repeated too often? Have you used three words where one will do? Take out anything that holds back the flow and rewrite.

Read your poem aloud. Does it sound clear and crisp? Can you hear its rhythm? Rewrite until you are satisfied with every word.

If you've listened to your poem, it will sing to you — it will move forward, reach a crescendo and take you to its finale.

Technique

Poets have many ways of making words come alive. Look for them in the poems you read and use them in your own writing. But don't overdo it! The following are some common language devices:

Simile	Makes a comparison using the words 'like' or 'as'.	*He was as grumpy as a ghost without a castle.* *The train charged down the track like a roaring dragon.*
Metaphor	An implied comparison between two different things. NB: Metaphors and similes both make comparisons, but in a metaphor the comparison is implied whereas in a simile it is indicated by 'like' or 'as'. For example, 'The sea of life' is a metaphor; 'Life is like a sea' is a simile.	*He had a heart of stone.* *An ant-file of uniformed students.* *Rainbow-bright friends, worth a pot of gold.*
Alliteration	The repetition of the same first letter or sound in a group of words.	*Swirling smoke spiralled up the stairs.*
Onomatopoeia	Words suggesting their meaning through descriptive sound.	*splash, click-clack, hiss, plop, buzz*
Personification	A lifeless object or idea is spoken of as if alive.	*Scraps of paper scuttled across the yard and hid in the long grass.*
Anthropomorphism	Animals, insects or birds are given human characteristics or feelings.	*The drab little sparrow longed for the brilliant plumage of the peacock.*
Repetition	Repeated use of a word, phrase or line.	*Nobody loves me* *Nobody cares* *Whenever I speak* *Nobody hears*

Haiku

Haiku is an ancient Japanese form of structured poetry. It's a challenge — and a useful exercise — to say a lot in a few words. Try it yourself. Usually haiku has a total of seventeen syllables: five in the first line, seven in the second, five in the third. The first and second lines lead to the main point made in the third line.

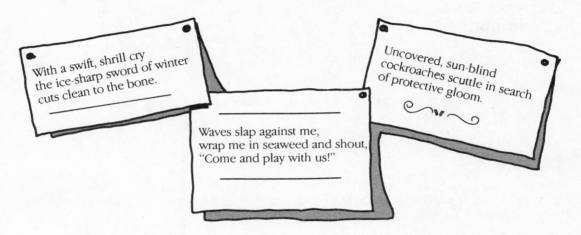

With a swift, shrill cry
the ice-sharp sword of winter
cuts clean to the bone.

Waves slap against me,
wrap me in seaweed and shout,
"Come and play with us!"

Uncovered, sun-blind
cockroaches scuttle in search
of protective gloom.

Further Resources

Ask a librarian for books on poetry reading and writing. The following titles may be useful:

On Poetry *by David Hill* (Heinemann)

Take a Risk — Trust Your Language, Make a Poem *by Michael P Harlow* (Christchurch Teachers' College)

DRAMA

When you are play-acting, sticks can become swords, boxes are fortresses, and strips of material are transformed into flowing robes. It's not just a game — it's real, alive, exciting — it's **drama.**

See It

When you write a play, try to picture a stage in your mind. Watch your characters move and speak.

Conflict

Make sparks fly between your characters. Real life is full of conflict; conflict is the life force of drama.

Outline

As with most writing, it's important to plot a shape for your play.

1. A strong opening will catch your audience's attention. Introduce the characters as early as possible or have them mentioned by name.
2. The plot thickens. Action and conflict between your characters builds dramatic tension. Keep the story moving.

3. The climax will be the high point. It's the explosive moment when the conflict really flares.
4. Tie it all together. Remember — endings don't have to be happy-ever-after but they should be satisfying.

Pace

Follow a lively scene with a quieter moment. To keep excitement at fever pitch will exhaust your audience. Give them a breather every now and then but keep the storyline flowing.

Contrast Characters

Give your characters different personalities which will provide the opportunity for natural interaction. Look at your own class at school and notice the contrast between the quiet, shy pupils and the talkative, energetic ones. Then there's the happy, good-natured students and the grumpy, discontented ones.

Character Growth

Through your storyline, challenge your main characters, give them problems to face, have them change and grow.

Conversation

Your characters are telling the story by what they say. Don't waste words — be direct — and keep the conversation flowing.

You can introduce background information through questions, e.g.,
> *"What happened to you?"*

Move the story forward by giving directions, e.g.,
> *"See who's at the door."*

Set the scene for future happenings, e.g.,
> *"I don't know how we'll manage now I've lost my job."*

How your characters speak reveals a lot about their personalities. Quite different people will say, "Hello" or "Good afternoon" or "G'day" or "Hi" or "Kia ora". Study people and listen to how they speak. Be wary of foreign accents as they are difficult to manage and maintain.

Silence

Silence can be effective. At a tense part of the play it can be very dramatic to stop all action and sound for a moment.

Movement

Give your characters a reason for moving, e.g., helping an elderly person to stand or hunting for a lost object. Movement should show something about a character or help the story along in some way. Ensure that actors stand where they can be seen by the audience, and that they do not face the back of the stage when speaking as this muffles the voice.

Time Span

Keep your story within a natural flow of time. Large jumps backwards and forwards in time are difficult to follow.

Audience Involvement

Consider audience participation. You may invite your audience to take part in a sing-along or join in a response of some sort. You might ask them questions or riddles. You could even set your drama in a court room where the audience becomes the jury.

Setting

Whether you set your play at a disco or a bus stop, avoid complicated set changes by having all the scenes situated in one place. Sketch a floor plan — mark entrances and exits. Obviously an inside setting like a classroom, hospital, prison or kitchen is simple to plan. However, a few rocks, a tent or shrubs in pots will convey an outside scene.

* You may use different levels for your setting by having platforms around the stage set. For good effect, curtain them off until your characters are ready to use them.
* You may have your audience sitting around the stage in a circle or semi-circle as at a circus.
* Surprise your audience occasionally by having an actor enter from behind them or come down from the stage into the audience.

Music

Music is a powerful mood-setter. Play a theme song or melody to highlight important moments. Songs or rhymes can bring a lively rhythm to your play. Chants give a mystical or spooky mood.

* Drums make good thunder; a single recorder can convey haunting sounds of the sea; half coconut shells clapped together sound like horses' hooves.

Lighting

You may be fortunate to have your play staged in a theatre with theatrical lighting to add atmosphere. Otherwise you will have to make do with curtains, room lights and torches.

Costumes

Hats or masks are sometimes all that's needed to create a character. Old sheets and curtains can be cut up to make a variety of costumes — capes, robes, ghostly garments, etc.

Colour is important. Use bold, vivid colours for excitement; dark, sombre colours for a serious mood. Contrast colours — don't set black clothes against a black stage curtain unless this is done deliberately to achieve a spooky effect.

Venue

Plays can be performed in parks, streets, shopping malls or playgrounds. When outside, use a simple plot, bright costumes, lots of movement and it is a good idea to involve the audience.

Themes

Historical - Bring to life past events in history. Read everything you can about the event and imagine what the people would say and do. Be dramatic!

Traditional - Dramatise familiar tales like *Chicken Licken*. Modernise the story by having present-day children go to tell the Prime Minister that the sky is falling down.

Cultural - Maori, Polynesian, Aborigine and other indigenous people have many customs and rituals which are spectacular and beautiful. Research these events thoroughly to absorb their full meaning. Some of the ceremonies are sacred so you must be careful not to give offence.

Mythical - This, too, is steeped in culture and goes back thousands of years. Nevertheless, the great myths usually deal with human experience which doesn't change much. The stories make great drama.

Comical - Comedy covers a wide range from the knock-'em-down clown type to the dreamy character who constantly gets in a muddle amidst mounting confusion. Highlight the oddities of characters but keep them believable. Keep the plot moving. Conversation should be short and sharp. Do the unexpected — surprise your audience. Have a satisfactory climax, resolving all problems realistically.

NEWS WRITING

I keep six honest serving men,
(They taught me all I knew);
Their names are What and Why and When
And How and Where and Who.

Rudyard Kipling

"Hi! What's new?" is a common greeting and it captures the basic purpose of a reporter's work — to find out what's happening. The challenge is how to pass on that news in a short, honest and interesting way. Whether you are writing for a daily newspaper, a school bulletin or a monthly magazine, your article needs Kipling's six serving men: What, Why, When, How, Where and Who.

Structure

Begin with basic information.

> Kidney transplant patient, Nicola Purvis, was in great spirits at St Mary's Hospital today and doctors "had no particular worries", surgeon Vas Nehru said today at a meeting with the press.

WHO	Kidney transplant patient, Nicola Purvis
WHAT	was in great spirits
WHERE	at St Mary's Hospital
WHY	doctors "had no particular worries"
WHEN	today
HOW	at a meeting with the press

Supportive facts and information follow in order of importance, rather like an upside-down triangle divided into paragraph sections.

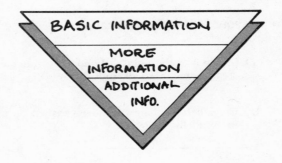

BASIC INFORMATION

MORE INFORMATION

ADDITIONAL INFO.

> Mr Nehru said that the operating team of surgeons, anaesthetists and nurses was very pleased with Nicola's progress.

Newspaper columns are narrow so keep sentences and paragraphs short.

Angle

Catch your reader's curiosity with your lead sentence.

a) Dragons are alive and well.

OR

b) Swimmers rushed from the water at Kulim Beach on Sunday afternoon.

Follow your lead with explanations:

a) Children at the library's holiday programme created dragons of all kinds.

b) Close behind them the waves washed up a mass of jellyfish.

Write Objectively

Write from an observer's point of view without the personal pronouns 'I' or 'me'.

Fact vs Opinion

It will be **fact** when a house burns down but only **opinion** as to how the fire started.

It will be **fact** when a swimmer wins a race but 'in record-breaking time' needs to be checked.

It will be **fact** when vandalism occurs at a school but suspicion is all that can be implied when reporting that 'a youth seen leaving the grounds is helping police with their enquiries.'

Eyewitness reports may be used to lend weight to theories. Where a statement cannot be checked as fact but is still newsworthy, it can be reported like this:

> Mrs Spratt believes the street's drinking water is polluted.

OR

> An observer said the UFO appeared to hover above the school.

OR

> In the opinion of an onlooker, the driver lost control of the vehicle.

Distortion

To change a person's words is dishonest. If a scientist says,

> "The world's food supply will run out in ten years if sensible crop-planning is not introduced."

and the newspaper headline reads,

SCIENTIST SAYS, "WORLD WILL SOON STARVE"

— that's distortion.

Identify

Say where your information came from, e.g.,

> Jane Blair, a college student, reported . . .
> The school's caretaker said . . .
> Research chemist, Beverley James, cautioned . . .

Make Sense

> Detective Fox found a rifle in the house which had been fired.

Really? Had the house been burned? If not, rewrite like this:

> In the house, Detective Fox found a rifle which had been fired.

Transition

Every phrase, sentence or paragraph should flow from the previous one and carry the reader smoothly from one thought or event to the next.

Some useful words to aid transition:

also
thus
since
likewise
however
another
meanwhile
accordingly
subsequently
furthermore

Helpful phrases:

In addition
for instance
for this reason
beyond this point

Redundancy

Some words are unnecessary, e.g.,

bare facts	*bare* can be left out
8 am in the morning	*in the morning* is unnecessary
fatal drowning	*fatal* is unnecessary
slightly small	*slightly* can be left out

Checklist

- Check correct spellings of names with the people themselves or reliable sources, e.g., MacDonald can also be written Macdonald or McDonald. Christian names also vary, e.g., Sonia, Sonja, Sonya.

- Check street names, towns or cities on maps.

- Check dates, days and times of events with someone in charge of the programme.

- Check on a calendar that days and dates match.

- Check titles, rank, etc., of persons who hold these.

- Check that you are using the correct spelling for words such as:

  stationary (motionless)
  stationery (paper etc.)
  mussel (shellfish)
  muscle (body tissue)
  coma (unconscious)
  comma (punctuation)

- Check exact meanings of words such as:

  amateur (non-professional)
  novice (beginner)
  infer (to deduce — applies to listener or reader)
  imply (to suggest — applies to speaker or writer)

The KISS Principle

This applies to all news reports.
KISS - *Keep It Short and Simple.*

FEATURE ARTICLES

Feature articles give detailed information on people or subjects.

Market Research

Identify your audience. Are you writing for a sporting, home-making, fashion or gardening magazine, etc.? Or is your article directed at readers of a local newspaper, etc.?

If your article is for a sporting magazine, suitable topics may be sporting personalities, correct care of equipment, personal fitness, dangerous elements of a particular sport, hints on performance, etc.

For a local newspaper suitable topics may include home safety, school holiday activities, interviews with interesting people, etc.

Topics suitable for a teenage magazine might be music, exercise, computers, camping, cooking, health, self-esteem, relationships, hobbies, budgeting, etc.

Human Interest

Issues that create strong public reaction make good feature articles. Research your article well, discover opposing points of view and try to find a fresh angle. For example, a lot has been written about punishment in schools but rarely are students asked what they think.

Quotes

Quotes from people bring your article to life and can support your point. More than one person may be quoted to give a balance of opinion or show a contrast. Be careful to quote honestly.

Length

Feature articles vary from between 1,000 to 2,500 words. Count the words in similar articles in the publication for which you are writing. Notice the sentence and paragraph lengths. Note the number of points made about a topic.

Annual Events

Editors welcome articles that give regular events a fresh slant, e.g.,

Easter in Antarctica
A Policeman's Christmas
Orphanage Celebrates Mother's Day

Titles

An editor has the right to choose all headlines. Nevertheless, if your title is bright and snappy it could be accepted. Keep it short and to the point.

Lights Out   *(article on children's bedtimes)*
Stretch and Bend   *(exercise article)*
Writing Rules — OK?   *(helpful writing hints)*

Checkpoint

Ask yourself
- Does your opening catch the eye?
- Who will care about your subject?
- Does your article say anything new?
- Are your points clear and crisp?
- Is your article ALIVE — or deadly dull?

INTERVIEWS

When someone new joins your class or club, they are usually asked a lot of questions, e.g., Where do you come from? Why did you come here? How old are you? Do you have any brothers or sisters? Do you play any sport? The conversation will be aimed at finding out about the new person. That same curiosity is the key to good interviews.

Preparation

Contact the person you wish to interview by writing to them or telephoning. Say who you are and why you would like to interview them.

No matter whom you are interviewing, do some **research** first. For example, if you are interviewing an elderly woman about her childhood, first read about the era in which she grew up. Note the differences in transport, schools, food, work, housing, church, etc. Such background information can help you to prompt her to remember these things and how they affected her life, along with any special joys or hardships she can recall.

Plan a list of questions. Ask the what, why, when, how, where and who questions. Put them in order by dealing with one topic at a time.

The Interview

- Make an appointment. Never just say you'll come round "some time on Monday" — make an actual time to call and be punctual.

- Take care with your appearance. A neat, well-organised reporter will give the impression of someone capable of doing a good job.

- Take a note pad and at least two pens. If you are using a tape recorder, take spare batteries and tapes. **Caution**: some people don't like being recorded — ask permission first.

- Chat first. Relax and make the person being interviewed feel comfortable with you.

- Listen to what the person is saying to you.

- Follow up on interesting points the person makes.

- Be interested — if you are really listening, your interest will show and the person will talk more easily.

- Never interrupt. It's bad manners and can make the person lose an important train of thought.

- Take note of what the person is wearing, your surroundings and any other interesting details.

- Quotes must be accurate. Record or write down exactly what is said.

- Don't rush the interview — you might miss hearing something worthwhile.

- Respect privacy. Don't write about anything told to you in confidence.

Writing Up Your Notes

As soon as possible, rewrite your notes while they are fresh in your mind. Include all the details that you can remember. If you have used a tape recorder you will need to transcribe it. That is, to play back the tape and note points about the interview, taking care that all direct quotes are accurate.

Writing the Article

Sort all your information and notes into a beginning, middle and end. A good way to start your article is with a quote from the person interviewed. For example:

"When Coral started to walk we had her tethered by a rope to a crowbar."

Follow up with details:

Mary Brotherston raised her family in a tent on the banks of a swift river.

Your earlier research will add to the body of your article. Quotes will help make it come alive. If you need more information about the person interviewed, ask his/her family or friends for their comments. In your article mention these people separately:

A longtime friend says of Mary, "She's a hard worker and never one for complaining."

Thank You

When your story is finished, send a copy to the person interviewed with a letter of thanks.

ADVERTISEMENTS

Advertisements take the place of the town crier of yesteryear, that is, telling people what's happening in the community and where to buy or sell goods and services.

Advertising space is expensive, so the message must be short, clear and crisp. Decide whom you want to read your advertisement and place it in a suitable market. If you have a canoe for sale, try the local newspaper's Boats for Sale column, the school notice board or a boating club's newsletter.

The following are a few examples of different types of advertisement.

Work Wanted

Babysitting Service: Experienced, reliable college student available for weekend and evening babysitting. Good references. Phone Phil, 752-370, after 4 p.m.

Odd Jobs: Hard-working, honest teenager willing to tackle any work, inside or outside. Reasonable hourly rate. Phone Ray: 62-485.

For Sale

Garage Sale: Bargains in sports equipment, trendy clothes, records, camping gear, etc. Come at 9 a.m., Saturday 13th, to 87 Dome Street.

Bicycle: Lady's ten-speed road bicycle. New tires and seat, good condition. Two years old. Phone 58-743.

Public Notices

Writers: Are you interested in joining a writing group? Beginners or experienced writers, poets, authors, hopefuls and scribblers — come to the Arts and Crafts Centre, Wharf Street, on Monday 15 July at 7 p.m. For further information, phone Sam, 761-292.

RADIO

Radio forms pictures in the mind — the words used enable the listeners to create their own images. Tune in to radio talks, stories and plays. Listen carefully. Notice what works well and why.

Talks

1 **Catch your listener**. The lead sentence should rivet their attention. Your listener may be at work, studying or dozing, etc. Your aim is to make them sit up and feel that you are talking directly to them. Get their attention by first asking a question, e.g., "Are we in danger of losing our sense of smell?"

2 **Follow up with the point of your topic.** In this instance, "Air fresheners, air extractor fans and range hoods are robbing us of smells."

3 **Keep your listener interested.** Expand your idea with a fresh approach, keep it lively and moving forward all the time.

4 **Speak clearly.** Whatever is broadcast must be understood immediately. A listener can't ask, "What did you say?" or replay a certain sentence.

5 **Choose words carefully.** Use plain, direct language, and keep your sentences short and to the point.

6 **Avoid confusing statistics.** If numbers or statistics are important to the talk, keep them brief and well spaced out.

7 **Take one fact at a time.** Work smoothly from one point to the next.

8 **Avoid catch phrases or clichés.** Stay away from phrases such as 'let's face it' or 'so to speak'.

9 **Identify people before quoting them.** State occupation first, then name, e.g., "The Mayor of Doomsville, Mr Noel Blight, said . . .". Quotes should be brief.

10 **Encourage reflection.** Leave your listeners thinking about your topic by closing your talk with something like, "Turn off those whirring fans, throw out the aerosol cans and go for a walk in the country."

Timing: One hundred words will equal approximately one minute of radio time. Talks may vary between two and fifteen minutes. Time the talks you hear on the radio.

Writing Your Talk: Write as you would speak. Read it aloud. Listen. Record your talk if possible. Are the sentences short and easily understood? Do the words sound clear or do they slide together? Do you run out of breath mid-sentence? Is there a rhythm or does it sound jerky?

Radio Drama

Storyline, plot, conflict and development are as important for radio drama as they are for short stories or theatre. What is different for this medium, however, is the necessity to draw word pictures of the setting and to tell listeners about the characters.

Characters must be quite different from each other in what they say and how they sound. Male and female, and child and adult characters make good contrasts. Limit the number of characters used. More than three or four actors can be confusing.

The setting is shown to the listener through the conversation of characters:

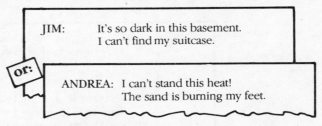

JIM: It's so dark in this basement.
         I can't find my suitcase.

or:

ANDREA: I can't stand this heat!
         The sand is burning my feet.

The plot (problem to be solved) should be introduced early in the story:

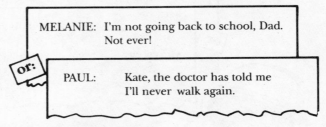

MELANIE: I'm not going back to school, Dad.
          Not ever!

or:

PAUL: Kate, the doctor has told me
          I'll never walk again.

Sound effects can help illustrate what is happening:

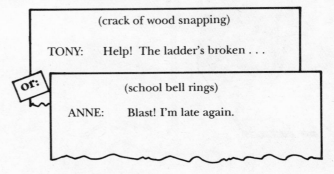

(crack of wood snapping)

TONY: Help! The ladder's broken . . .

or:

(school bell rings)

ANNE: Blast! I'm late again.

Music can help set the mood or atmosphere:

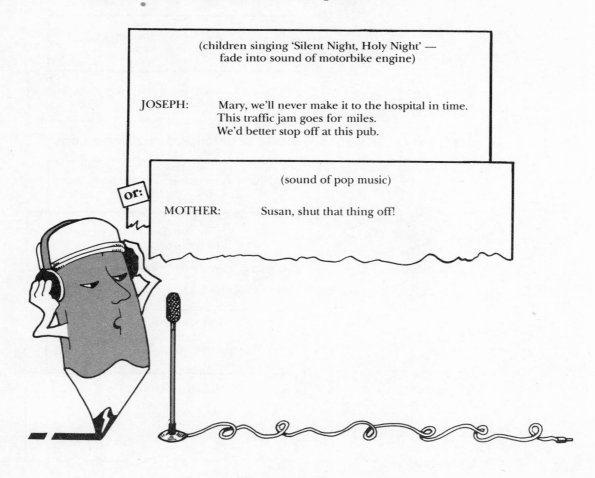

(children singing 'Silent Night, Holy Night' —
fade into sound of motorbike engine)

JOSEPH: Mary, we'll never make it to the hospital in time.
This traffic jam goes for miles.
We'd better stop off at this pub.

or:

(sound of pop music)

MOTHER: Susan, shut that thing off!

TELEVISION

Good television has suspense, conflict, tension, drama and development. If you have an idea that you feel will make an excellent television program, first you should write out a synopsis.

Synopsis

This is an outline of your story idea, characters and setting. Three or four pages typed in double spacing will tell a producer whether your idea has merit. Keep your cast numbers small. Use simple settings — indoor settings are easiest to produce. Olden-day costumes are expensive, so try to set your story in the present.

If a producer likes your synopsis you will be asked to develop it further.

Hints

1   **Think visually.** Turn down the sound on your television and watch the characters. Try to discover what is happening from what you see. When you are writing, think about the pictures you see in your mind.

2   **Keep dialogue to a minimum.** Good actors will show their emotions by expressions and movements.

3   A good device to use occasionally is to **contrast what a character says by showing them doing the opposite.**

For example:

DENNIS: Bye, Mum! I'm off to school now.

Dennis walks outside, turns the
corner and runs off into the park,
in the opposite direction to school.

(Production details are written on the left side of the paper with dialogue on the right.)

PROCESS WRITING

This covers the process of writing from the idea to the completed piece. The order of progress is usually like this:

Pre-writing
- Deciding what to write about
- Considering your approach to the topic
- Discussion
- Research
- Note-taking
- Planning the order of subject development

Writing
- Draft writing of first copy
- Revision of writing
- Polishing and editing
- Writing good copy

Post-writing
- Proof reading (see p. 60)
- Binding work into its finished form
- Sharing
- Reader's response

BOOK REVIEWS

When you are given a book to review, read it through fully
without skipping any parts. Then skim through it again and note:

* **Main characters**
* **Setting**
* **Summary of the plot or theme**
* **Parts you liked**
* **Parts you found disappointing**

Ask yourself some questions:

- Did the characters come alive for you?
- Was the action well planned?
- Could you picture the setting?
- Did the plot drag on?
- Were there any confusing parts?
- Was the ending believable and satisfying?
- Did you enjoy the book?

Note certain things about the book's production:

- Is the type easy to read?
- Are the illustrations well done and do they suit the story?
- Is the index helpful?
- Are there a lot of printing errors?
- Is the book easy to hold?
- Is it well bound?

Now put your notes in order and write your review. Give book information at the start, e.g.,

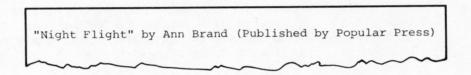

```
"Night Flight" by Ann Brand (Published by Popular Press)
```

Give good reasons for your comments and be fair with criticism. Outline the characters and plot but don't give away the ending. Say who you think might enjoy the book, e.g., young readers, or 10-12 year olds.

Some books will give information about the author which can also be summarised in your review.

PROJECTS

Research

Hunt out all the information you can find on your topic. Look in encyclopaedia, borrow library books, ask parents for help, check newspaper files, or even ask at travel agencies, etc., for booklets on other countries.

Order

Arrange your information. Jot down subject headings on small cards and on these write down where you've found the information. Number the cards in order of usefulness. Mark books with slips of paper and write a key phrase to the information contained within on top of these slips.

Plan Your Project

Ideas:

- Design a front cover.
- Draw a map. Write a 'Fascinating Facts' page.
- Imagine you are living at the time or place of your topic — write a diary of one week of your life. Describe where you live, your family and friends, games, chores, food, etc.
- Write a radio or newspaper report of an important event.
- Write a poem.
- Review a book about your subject.
- Draw portraits of people in your project. Note details about their clothing or physical appearance.

- Write a weather report of the time.
- Make a tourist brochure.
- Make a contents page listing each item included in your project.
- When the project is complete, number the pages and fill in the corresponding numbers on the contents page.
- Design a bold, clear heading for each new item in your project.

EXPOSITORY ESSAY

This type of essay explores and exposes your ideas on an issue. It needs:

★ *careful planning and research,*

★ *clear expression of ideas,*

★ *sound points of argument,*

★ *accurate details.*

Jot down all the ideas that come to mind about your topic. Put them in 'For' and 'Against' columns. Decide whether your viewpoint will be 'For' or 'Against'.

Arrange your ideas in order of importance. Your first paragraph will contain your main topic or argument. Decide what ideas should go in your middle paragraphs and number them. Conclude with a persuasive paragraph.

Introduction

The first paragraph outlines your approach to the issue. It should be clearly written and capture a reader's interest.

Development

Like news writing, your points should follow in logical order. All facts should follow in order of importance, rather like an upside-down triangle divided into paragraph sections.

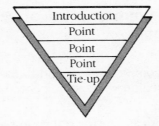

Each paragraph deals with only one idea and contains all the necessary information. Don't ramble or preach. Vary the lengths of your sentences to avoid becoming boring. Link paragraphs with connective phrases such as:

In addition,   As evidence,   On the contrary,   Equally important . . .

Conclusion

Recap briefly your initial point. Convince the reader that your reasoning is sound. Sum up strongly, perhaps beginning:

Therefore,   Consequently,   As a result . . .

SUMMARY OR PRECIS

The purpose of a summary is to condense a passage of writing into the main points.

- Read through the complete piece and think about its meaning. Re-read at least once more. Decide what is the central subject.

- List the important ideas, leaving out examples and other information. Use only essential data.

- Be careful not to alter the original meaning. If the passage is written as someone's opinion, make that point clear. For example: Scientist Arthur Dean believes people can survive nuclear winter.

- Think about the key points and rewrite them into one paragraph using your own words.

- Read your paragraph carefully. Does it make sense? Do your sentences flow logically from one point to another?

- Revise your paragraph. Cut out unnecessary words or repetitions. When you are satisfied with your summary, rewrite it.

- Count the number of words and note them at the bottom of the page.

An example of a precis may be, for the story of 'The Gingerbread Man':

The Gingerbread Man - a traditional tale

An elderly woman without children of her own bakes a gingerbread man who, when he is taken out of the oven, jumps up and runs away. Chased by the woman, her husband and others along the way, the gingerbread man becomes trapped at a river where a fox offers to carry him across. The gingerbread man jumps onto the fox's nose and the fox eats him.

(66 words)

PROOF READING

When you have completed the first rough copy of your work:

1   Read it through carefully.

2   Check the spelling of words you don't use very often — have you spelt names and places correctly? Check to make sure.

3   Do your sentences make sense? Attention to punctuation may be all that's needed. (See Punctuation, page 80)

4   Are your facts jumbled together? Space them out so they are easy to read.

5   Have you repeated some words several times? Use a thesaurus to discover variations.

6   Write out your good copy.

7   Read it through carefully and correct any mistakes.

read

check

correct

re-read

PREPARING A MANUSCRIPT

Good presentation of your work will go a long way towards showing an editor that your script is worth reading. Tatty manuscripts, littered with cross-outs and untidy additions, will soon be tossed on the rejection pile, often unread.

- Manuscripts are best typed in double spacing on one side of the paper. Leave at least one-inch margins at each side and leave space at both the top and bottom of the pages. Number each page at the top right-hand side, and refer to the title, e.g., Christmas . . . p.3.

- All manuscripts should have a cover page, possibly set out like so:

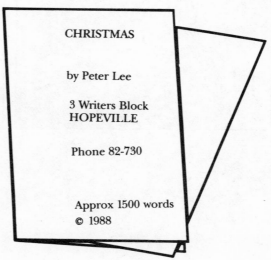

CHRISTMAS

by Peter Lee

3 Writers Block
HOPEVILLE

Phone 82-730

Approx 1500 words
© 1988

- Some writers enclose a letter offering the script for the editor's consideration.

- Always enclose a stamped, self-addressed envelope for the return of your manuscript. If you are posting it overseas, you can buy International Reply Coupons at a Post Office.

- Use an envelope large enough to fit your manuscript in without folding.

- Remember, lost manuscripts are not the responsibility of the publisher. Always retain a photocopy yourself.

SPEECHES

After you've seen a good movie a friend may ask you, "How was it?" and you launch into an excited description. Or perhaps a new student asks you how to find the principal's office and you give directions. Both of these responses carry the elements of speechmaking. Lively description, accurate details and hand gestures highlighting certain points. Unfortunately, good speeches don't happen quite so easily; they are the result of careful planning and thought.

Some points to remember

★ **Who** is your audience? Choose your topic so that it will interest the people listening. Ask yourself, before deciding, if they would prefer a talk on canaries, cricket or camping . . .?

★ **A snappy opening** is needed to convince your audience that you are worth listening to.

★ The body of your talk will be filled out by **good planning and research.**

★ Remember, you are holding a **conversation** with people so you need to write your words as you would speak.

★ **Humour** often helps to make a point as well as maintaining your audience's interest but be careful not to make fun of anyone.

★ **Be sensitive** — don't resort to sarcasm or personal criticism.

★ **Quotes** from other people can add interest and credibility to your talk. Keep them short.

★ **Conclusion** — you should refer to your opening sentence in some way and finish on a strong note.

Preparation

Time your speech to be sure it fits into the slot allowed. Record it if possible.
Edit your talk. Have you rambled on? Have you repeated the same words often? Does it flow? Does it make sense? Either expand it or cut it as necessary.
Memorise your talk if you can. Onto small cards that fit into your hand, jot down the main points of your speech and some key words to jog your memory.

Visual Aids

Select a few items to add interest to your speech. If you intend to use maps and graphs, make sure they are large enough to be seen by everyone and check before you start that there is somewhere to hang them. If you use an overhead projector or slide camera, make sure the equipment is working and that you know how to use it. Keep all visual aids out of sight until you are ready to show them.

Delivery

1   **Appearance** — how you look will be the first thing an audience notices.
2   **Posture** — walk calmly to the speaker's platform and stand with feet slightly apart and your arms relaxed at your sides.
3   **Relax** by taking a deep breath and let it out slowly.
4   **Address** your audience; e.g., "Good afternoon, everyone."
5   **Voice** — imagine you are speaking to the person right at the back of the room. Keep your head up and your voice will carry better. Don't rush your speech. Try to maintain a rhythm and vary it now and then. Pause after an important point to give it more effect.
6   **Eye contact** — look *at* people. If your speech is not too serious, smile occasionally.

LETTER WRITING

Everyone likes to receive a letter but writing a reply is often an effort. "I don't know what to say," is a common cry.

It helps to start with the right materials:

- Standard-size, lined (or unlined with a guide sheet) white paper is suitable for all types of letters. Save the fancy prints or bright colours for casual letters to friends.

- A black or blue pen.

- Post Office standard-size envelopes.

- Postage stamps (if you do not put enough postage on your letter, the recipient may be charged extra).

Personal Letter

A personal letter
is usually set out like this:

205 Bourke Street
Merivale
CHRISTCHURCH 1
22 November 1988

Dear Catherine

I enjoyed reading your last letter and I'm pleased your arm is out of plaster – now you won't have to worry about keeping it dry in the shower.

Yes, I entered the school swimming sports again this year and made it into the semi-finals of the backstroke. I ran out of steam towards the end, though, so missed out on the final. Are you playing a sport this year?

I'm sorry, I can't find the book you thought you'd left here last holidays. I've even cleaned out my cupboard! Do you think you could have left it on the bus?

Thanks for the news about Jeff. Please say hi from me next time you see him. Do you remember Jenny? Her family are moving to Riverton next month and she's upset at having to leave all her friends here and start a new school.

Well, Mum's calling me to wash the dishes now and then we're off to the library so I guess I better sign off now.

Best Wishes
Linda

The letter above answers all the questions that Catherine asked in her last letter, then asks some of her. It also fills her in on what's been happening with Linda's family and friends.

Thank You Letters

Be polite and grateful but don't gush!

Dear Grandma

Your Address
Date

Thank you for being so thoughtful and remembering my birthday.

How did you guess I needed a new T-shirt? It fits very well and the colour goes with most of my shorts and jeans. Mum says it looks really nice on me.

I hope you are planning to visit soon. You won't recognise our puppy when you do, he's grown so much!

Lots of love

Sympathy Letters

These are difficult to write. Be sincere. Mention a personal memory you have of the person who died. Include your address and sign your surname as well as your Christian name.

Your Address
Date

Dear Mrs Ferrar

I was very sorry to hear of your husband's death. Mr Ferrar gave a lot of pleasure to the neighbourhood. My friends and I enjoyed his tales of the old days, and he grew the best strawberries on the block

I will call on you later in the week to see if there are any messages or chores you would like help with.

Yours sincerely

Business Letters

Be brief and use plain language. Check that spelling of names and the address is correct. If you're not sure whether the person you're writing to is male or female, address them by their occupational title, e.g., Dear Principal.

```
                                            Your Address
                                            Date


         The Manager
         Bookworm Publishers
         PO Box 106
         AUCKLAND 1

         Dear Manager

         I would like to buy a copy of 'Ride the River'
         as advertised in the latest issue of Book Review.

         I have enclosed a money order for $5.95 in
         payment.

         Yours faithfully

         L. D. Firth
```

Note that if you are writing a business letter to someone whose name you do not know, always close with 'Yours faithfully'. If you know the person's name and have begun 'Dear Mr So-and-So', close with 'Yours sincerely'.

Letters to the Editor

Write about some local issue that concerns you. You could comment on a previously published item that you either agree or disagree with. Letters of praise are rare but make a pleasant change, if sincere. Some publications allow pen names (e.g., Confused, Scorpio, etc.) to be published with letters, but you must still sign your real name and include your address.

Your address
Date

Dear Editor

Why is it that the City Council is planning to tear down the adventure playground in Central Park and build a ten-pin bowling alley in its place?

There are no other open playgrounds anywhere near the city centre and for us children who live in small apartments and houses without back yards, we like to play at the park. A ten-pin bowling alley won't be much use for us because we won't be allowed to play around there, and we can't afford to go bowling all the time.

It's important to us to have somewhere to meet and play outside. Perhaps the City Council hasn't heard that 'Parks are for People'.

Yours faithfully

Letters of Complaint

Never write a letter while angry; you may later regret any harsh words. Time sometimes solves the problem or you may think of a better way to deal with it. If not, be factual and polite.

The Production Manager
Regal Recordings Ltd
63-65 Brookmount Street
St Clair
DUNEDIN

Dear Manager

I am very disappointed in the poor quality of the enclosed cassette, 'Heavenly'. The tape's packaging was sealed when I bought it so the fault must have occurred during production.

The record shop where I bought the cassette will not exchange it or refund my money but the manager, Mr Logan, gave me your address.

I would appreciate it if you would give this matter your attention.

Yours faithfully

Ken Davidson

Ken Davidson

Job Application

11 High Street
HAWERA
10 August 1989

Mrs Susan Adamson
Manager
Thrifty Grocery Store
Cnr Bond & Roy Streets
HAWERA

Dear Mrs Adamson

   I would like to apply for the position of after-school delivery person as advertised in this morning's Daily Herald.

   I am a 12-year-old student, a willing and responsible worker, and I have my own bicycle. Please ring me (Ph. 34-178) if you would like me to come in for an interview.

Yours sincerely

Ray Roberts

Ray Roberts

Envelopes

Centre the person's name and address in the bottom half of the envelope. The stamp should be stuck in the top right-hand corner. Write *your* name and address on the top left-hand corner or the back flap of the envelope so the letter can be returned to you if it is undelivered.

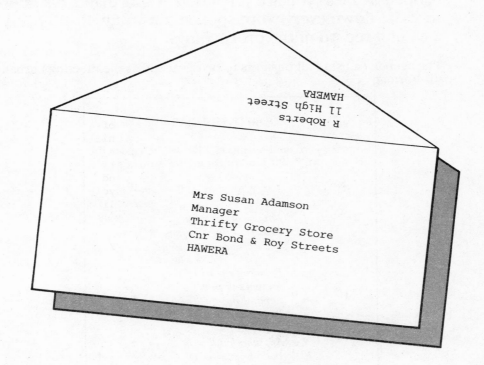

MEETING REPORTS

Taking the minutes of a meeting means writing a report of what happens. Unless you are very good at shorthand, it's impossible to write down every word spoken but you will still need to keep a careful record of the proceedings.

The agenda (a list of all business to be discussed at the meeting) usually follows this format:

BOOKLOVERS' CLUB

A meeting of the Booklovers' Club will be held at the Henderson Public Library, Saturday 5 April at 2 pm.

A G E N D A

1. *Minutes of last meeting*
2. *Matters arising therefrom*
3. *Correspondence — inward*
   — outward
4. *Financial report*
5. *Annual subscriptions*
6. *Fundraising*
7. *Lost property*
8. *Christmas tree*
9. *Any other business*
10. *Date of next meeting*

Generally, a meeting will proceed along the following lines, and minutes should be written up in the same order:

Minutes of a Meeting of the Booklovers' Club
held at Henderson Public Library, Saturday 5 April 1988 at 2 pm

The Convener opened the meeting at (note the time).

Present
If it is a small group, list everyone's name. If it is a large crowd, record the names of committee members present and estimate the number of others attending the meeting.

Apologies
People who can't be at the meeting will usually have asked someone to have their apologies recorded.

Minutes of Previous Meeting
The Secretary reads these then the Convener asks, "Will someone who was present at that meeting move that this is a true record of proceedings?" followed by, "Will someone second that motion?" Record like this:

It was moved that the minutes were a true record.
Moved: Jake Murray   Seconded: Trudi White

Business Arising from Minutes
If there has been any action taken since the previous meeting, or that has yet to be attended to, it will be discussed at this time and recorded in the minutes.

Correspondence
Inward:
The Secretary reads any letters received and these are discussed and recorded in the minutes.
Outward:
The minutes will record any decisions made about letters to be sent out either in reply to those received or regarding new business.

Financial Report
The Treasurer will present this, giving a detailed report on funds raised and money spent. Money matters need to be recorded accurately.

Business on the Agenda

Sub-headings:

Record the minutes of this section in the same order as the business is listed on the Agenda, with appropriate sub-headings.

How to record:

It is at this stage that your skills as a recorder will be put to the test. At meetings people sometimes speak very fast, or at the same time as somebody else. If you haven't heard someone clearly, ask the Convener to request the speaker to repeat what was said. If reports are read out, ask the convener to request a copy for the minutes. Sometimes, debate on an issue becomes general chitchat. The best you can do in this instance is to write something like, 'Discussion took place about . . .'

Motions:

After discussion, a *formal motion* is often put to the meeting. It should be recorded like this:

Gaylene Lee moved that the annual subscription fee be raised to $5.

Seconded: Billy Turner

The Convener asked for a show of hands.
For – 12; Against – 2. Motion carried.

Other examples:

Rebecca Bernstein volunteered to organise fund-raising for new books to be bought for the Children's Ward at the Public Hospital. Unanimously accepted.

The Convener asked Sam Wong to investigate lost property. He agreed.

Andrew Quinn asked that a Christmas tree be put in the library foyer. The Convener said she would attend to it.

Next Meeting

This date is usually decided at the meeting.

The Convener closed the meeting at (note time).

PEOPLE TALK

Some words like 'housewife' and 'foreman' indicate that only one sex is involved in the work. Other terms may be chosen to include both male and female, e.g., 'homemaker' and 'supervisor'.

Other alternatives:

chairman	convener
spokesman	representative
charwoman	cleaner
office girl	clerk/receptionist
manpower	workforce

Make up your own list of alternatives.

CONVENER

WRITERS' GROUPS

Form a writers' group at school or with your friends. Meet once or twice a month. Bring something new that you have written or that you have improved since the last meeting.

★ Read each other's work and offer *helpful* criticism. Comment on the parts you liked as well as what could be improved. Be supportive.

★ Set different subjects to write about to widen your field of writing.

★ Organise writing competitions. Ask a bookshop to donate prizes. Approach a local editor, writer or teacher to judge the entries and comment on them.

Guidelines for helpful criticism

Does the opening catch your attention? Do the characters come alive? Does the plot hold your interest? Are there any worn-out phrases or cliches? Is the setting clearly shown? Do the characters contrast and conflict? Does the dialogue sound natural? Does the main character develop? Is the end satisfying?

RECIPES

The following is the usual format for setting out a recipe. Always ensure that you give exact measurements and clear instructions. List the ingredients in the order used. If making up a new recipe, always test it yourself to make sure it's successful!

Common abbreviations used in recipes:

tsp (or t) — teaspoon   tbsp (or T) — tablespoon
g — grams   ml — millilitres

Yuletide Log

150 ml cream   1 heaped tsp cocoa
1 tbsp chocolate ice cream topping 1 packet chocolate chip cookies
1 heaped tsp icing sugar   tinfoil

Beat cream, ice cream topping, icing sugar and cocoa together until stiff but not lumpy. Divide the mixture in half, and use one half to spread on the biscuits, sandwiching them together on the tinfoil to form a long roll. Wrap biscuit log in foil and leave in refrigerator for 24 hours.

One hour before required, unwrap log and place on dish. Roughly spread the rest of the cream mixture over the log then pour a little chocolate topping over it. Replace in refrigerator until ready to serve. Slice on an angle.

PUNCTUATION

Good punctuation helps the reader to understand what the writer means. Here are some guidelines to the use of common punctuation. Remember, however, that there are always exceptions to the rule!

Comma (,)

A comma is used:

a) to separate words and phrases to make clear the meaning of a sentence. When reading aloud, pause at a comma.

b) to separate more than two adjectives, e.g.,

> The jacket was in a homespun, soft, pale green fabric.

c) to separate words in a list, e.g.,

> This item is available in blue, green, red, yellow or white.

d) to separate description and name, e.g.,

> The principal, Mrs James, announced the awards.
> Vic Molena, a spectator at the show, described the feat as breathtaking.

e) to separate numbers, e.g.,

> In 1980, 250 school canteens were inspected.

f) before and after direct speech, e.g.,

> Bronwyn said, "Hello." "Hello," said Steve.

g) to prevent misunderstanding, e.g.,

(i) The children who are wearing shoes will go on the hike.
(ii) The children, who are wearing shoes, will go on the hike.

The first sentence means that *only* those children wearing shoes will go on the hike. The second sentence means that all the children are going on the hike but adds the information that they're wearing shoes. In this case, if you remove the part of the sentence between the commas, it still means that all the children will go on the hike — a phrase that is incidental to the main point is placed between commas.

Full Stop, Period or Full Point (.)

a) A full stop is used at the end of a sentence, except where an exclamation mark or question mark is used instead.

b) It is also often used to indicate that a word has been abbreviated:

max.　maximum　　Aust.　Australia　　e.g.　*(exempli gratia)* for example

Semicolon (;)

A semicolon shows a separation not so complete as that shown by a full stop but greater than that shown by a comma. It is used:

a) **to separate subjects when commas alone do not make the meaning clear:**

Present at the Valley School assembly were: Mrs J. Collins, Principal; Mr S. Coster, Deputy Principal; Mr T Wells, Senior Teacher; Ms P. Nicol, Secretary; and several members of the school committee.

b) **where separate statements are linked together to show a relationship:**

In youth we believe many things; in old age we doubt many truths.

Colon (:)

A colon may be used:

a) **where a list or example follows:**

Bring to camp: sleeping bag, sturdy shoes, waterproof jacket, swimsuit, sweater, toilet bag, towel, two changes of clothes and underwear.

b) **before a formal quote:**

In the words of William Sansom: 'A writer lives, at best, in a state of astonishment.'

c) **to separate reference to Bible chapter and verse:**

Romans 11:33

d) **to separate book title and subtitle:**

In Step: Guidelines for Marching Teams

Exclamation Mark (!)

An exclamation mark is used:

a) **to stress a word or sentence:** Help! He did it!
b) **to show surprise:** Hey! Ah-ha!
c) **for a command:** Stop!

Question Mark (?)

Do you need to have a question mark explained?

Apostrophe (')

This is a form of punctuation with which a lot of people have trouble.
It generally shows possession or 'belonging to'.

a) **For the belongings of one person, put the apostrophe before the s:**

   Jane's bag, a child's ball, a writer's pen

   Impersonal pronouns also use an apostrophe before the s to show possession:

   anybody's desk, someone's book

   NB: Personal pronouns ***do not*** have an apostrophe when they end in s:

   yours, hers, theirs

b) **For the belongings of more than one person, put the apostrophe after the s:**

   a writers' group (i.e. a group for writers)

c) **Where the word itself is already plural, put the apostrophe before the s:**

   children's playground (a playground for children), old people's club (a club for old people)

d) **If the word already ends in s, add apostrophe s.**

   James's dog, St Thomas's church

e) **For classical names and qualities which end in s, add only an apostrophe:**

   Zeus' daughter, for goodness' sake

An apostrophe is also used for contractions, where figures or letters are left out:

'45 (1945)   o'er (over)   I'll (I will)   you're (you are)   it's (it is) *

*NB: Only use an apostrophe in 'it's' when it means 'it is', not when showing possession, e.g.,   *It's* chasing *its* own tail.

Brackets or Parentheses ( )

Brackets are used:

a) to enclose remarks made by the writer that are separate from the main statement:

Next week the class (and any parents who wish to) will visit a farm.

b) to insert an explanation not belonging to the main statement:

For centuries (no exact time is known) the treasure lay buried.

c) to give the botanical name of plants or animals:

the broadleaf (*Griselinia littoralis*), the starfish (*Astropecten*) . . .

Quotation or Speech Marks (" " or ' ')

Quotation marks are used:

a) **to enclose direct speech:** James said, "I will come back."

b) **for direct quotations from speech or written work:**

The Road Code states: "Where there is an adequate cycle track, use it."

If the above is written as an indirect quotation it would not require quotation marks:

The Road Code states that where there is an adequate cycle track it is to be used.

c) **around words or phrases that may be debatable:**

Many "experts" disagree.

or around words that have been made up for a particular purpose and which are not proper words:

That mixture has a wonderful "schloopiness" to it.

d) **If a quotation is made within direct speech, use single quotation marks inside double quotation marks:**

Mark said, "I don't know what 'pride goes before a fall' means."

Dash (—)

A dash shows an interruption stronger than the pause for a comma — use sparingly.

a)   Dashes may be used in pairs to enclose matter that could also be put in parentheses:

If this is true — and no one is sure that it is — we must do something about it.

b)   They may also be used singly to indicate a sharp break in a sentence:

"I can't see a thing in here — ouch!"

Hyphen (-)

The hyphen is used:

a)   to divide a word that doesn't fit at the end of a line. Check with your dictionary for the rules of word division, but some general rules are:

(i)   divide words between syllables (words of one syllable must never be split)

(ii) ensure that the pronunciation of the first part of the word is apparent before the eye reaches the second line (e.g., coincidence should be divided *co-incidence* to ensure that it is not confused with *coin-age*, etc.)

(iii) divide words between double consonants (e.g., com·mon) unless both consonants form the stem word (e.g., miss·ing).

b) **to prevent ambiguity:**

Consider the difference in meaning between 'The 20-odd members of the group' and 'The 20 odd members of the group'. Also, 'the deep-blue sea' and 'the deep, blue sea'.

c) **in composite adjectives *before* a noun:**

a six-metre-high wall; a 14-year-old girl

When these words *follow* the noun, hyphenation is not used:

a wall six metres high; a girl 14 years old

d) **Some other composite words are also hyphenated, e.g., merry-go-round, happy-go-lucky, grown-up, heart-to-heart. If you are unsure whether or not a word should be hyphenated, check it in your dictionary.**